Beautiful razor

love poems
and
other lies

Beautiful Razor© Al Hunter, 2012

Published by Kegedonce Press
11 Park Road, Cape Croker Reserve
R. R. 5, Wiarton, Ontario, N0H 2T0
www.kegedonce.com
Administration Office/Book Orders
RR7 Owen Sound, ON N4K 6V5

Copyeditor: Kateri Akiwenzie-Damm
Design: Red Willow Designs
Photo credits(cover & author portrait): Stephan Hoglund Photography
www.stephanhoglundphotography.com
Printed in Canada by Gilmore Printing Services, Ottawa, Ont.
Cover Printed on 10pt Kalima C1S
Text Printed on 160m Enviro 100 Satin

Library and Archives Canada Cataloguing in Publication

Hunter, Al, 1958-
    Beautiful razor : love poems & other lies / Al Hunter.

ISBN 978-0-9868740-1-7

    I. Title.

PS8565.U5767B43 2012   C811'.6   C2012-906345-2

Sales and Distribution - http://www.lpg.ca/LitDistco:
For Customer Service/Orders
Tel 1-800-591-6250 Fax 1-800-591-6251
100 Armstrong Ave. Georgetown, ON L7G 5S4
Email orders@litdistco.ca

Kegedonce Press gratefully acknowledges the generous support of:

ONTARIO ARTS COUNCIL
CONSEIL DES ARTS DE L'ONTARIO

*We acknowledge the support of the Canada Council for the Arts which last
year invested $20.1 million in writing and publishing throughout Canada.*

Canada Council   Conseil des Arts
for the Arts   du Canada

Love Poems

Contents

Other Lies

"Love is a four letter word like poem."
— Mike Hazard

"Let me feel, let me feel what I'm feeling tonight."
— Serena Ryder

"You don't always have to chop with the sword of truth.
You can point with it too."
— Anne Lamott

"The knife got near my throat again."
— Charles Bukowski

MEMORIAM

Adriana Arango
July 14, 1976 – July 21, 2011
Medellin, Colombia
Estimada hermana, siempre una estrella en mi
cielo, para siempre en mi corazón.

Acknowledgements

One morning, we wake, we make it through; we break through the most destitute and bereft times of our lives. Grief and longing dissipate a little more. We move on.

To my children and grandchildren, I return the unconditional love and acceptance you give me.

To my friends and relatives, I return the unconditional love and acceptance you give me.

I mention and thank, Stephan Hoglund, a kindred spirit and brother for an unbelievable amount of support and love over the years. Miigwech, Stephan, also, for the cover photography and portrait for this book.

To my brother-in-arms & compatriot, Rod McLeod, I say, miigwech, for encouraging me to always carry on.

Thank you, Montana Picard, for knowing when to reach out. Thanks for being one of the best friends I have. To dear friend, Pam Nahgahnub and family, thanks for always being there and making available a safe refuge when I need one. To Kimberley Wilde, I have not enough words to express the depth of my thanks and gratitude for your wise and much needed counsel and friendship over the years. Thank you, my friend, Frank Koehn, for sharing your strength and laughter. Keith Secola, your words and support, are always music to my ears.

Of course, I thank my sis, Irene, for reminding me to remain open-minded and compassionate, and for being available when needed the most.

Many other people have supported me over the years and still do. Namely, Allison Adele Hedge Coke, Heid Erdrich, Lise Erdrich, Louise Erdrich, Denise Lagimodiere, Bill & Edye Howes & family, Sarah Agaton-Howes, Jim & Pat Northrup, Ivy Vainio, Michael "Waabi" Furo, David Hopkins, Mary Alice Smith & Joe Morrison, Omar Perez, Emerson Tabares Gomez, Catalina Castellano Moreno, Adriana Arango, Musa Abdel-Rahman, Winona LaDuke, Faye Brown, Teresa Bertossi, Joan Farnam, Katherena Vermette and the gang at the Aboriginal Writers Collective of Manitoba, Tracy Neilson-Brown, Eleanor Skead & Bert Landon, Lynn & Lucien Aubin, Sally Skead, Tim Archie, Teresa Hazel, Stan Vlotaros, Nicole Cochrane, Karen McCall, & Elvis Debungee.

Thank you, Paul Seesaquasis, for your editorial acumen and friendship. Mostly, thank you, Kateri and Renee, for everything related to publishing this book, for supporting Aboriginal writers, and for being compassionate & loving spirits. You are both amazing, honest, straight-forward, and kind.

Love Poems

At Our Tender Age

We lost our soul mates
To the illusory and untrue
It was no one's fault
You were but a girl
I was but a boy
Lost in middle-age
A trajectory
That began at early loss and grief
Through trauma and the unresolved
Until the innocence gave way to negligence and lassitude
As we stumbled through the jagged and the numb
You, to the dark melange of bars and empty lovers
I, to the darkness of mental destitution and dissociation
We are the same
You, but a girl
I, but a boy
Lost in middle-age
May we someday return to our healing
To the embrace of hummingbirds and horses
To the shelter of stars and constellations
May we be guided
You, a woman
I, a man
Back to our place of souls
Back to where we belong.

Beautiful Razor

It is useless to shield my jugular

I offer up my throat
A forgone conclusion

I offer my silent thanks
To the sharpening strap

The object of our mutual affection

The razor and mine

I talked with the moon

I talked with the moon tonight
I asked her for a favour
I asked her to cover you
I asked her to visit your home
I asked her to visit your waters
To take love and forgiveness
To dip it in moonlight
To offer it to you
And once you had enough
To remind you,
"He is thirsty, too."

The Rain Fell

The rain was love.
You were the earth.
The rain fell, as did I.

Blue Rain

I live in this empty house of the sun
A vessel into which blue rain falls.

It was my mistake

It was my mistake to think that we could return to the shores
That we once loved

It was my mistake to think that we could return to the streams
That once tangled and rolled

It was my mistake to think that we could return to the rivers
That once roared with love

It was my mistake to think that we could return to find the stones
That we left behind

It was my mistake to think that we could return to the coves
That kept our secrets

It was my mistake to think that we could return to yesterday's skies
That reflected in water

It was my mistake to think that we could return to light the fire
That had grown cold

It was my mistake to think that we could return to find flowers
That grew in winter

It was my mistake to think that we could return to the miles
Already gone

It was my mistake to think that we could…

I watched the world fall away

I watched the world fall away
Gravity could not keep me tethered to you
Adrift, the safe light of stars escaped me.

Once I passed close to the crescent moon
My reach was not enough

Once I passed close to Venus
My reach was not enough

I watched the world fall away
Gravity could not keep me tethered to you
Adrift, I am without you.

Goodbye to this Hurt Town

Goodbye to this Hurt Town
My heart isn't rent to own
Pain is in the squeaky floors
It's peeling off the walls
It's wailing through the open doors
I won't be taking your calls

"I'm done," read
Her message in a bottle
Go on then, darling, go on
I'm saying goodbye to this Hurt Town

Goodbye to this Hurt Town
My heart isn't rent to own
Pain is in the squeaky floors
It's peeling off the walls
It's wailing through the open doors
I won't be taking your calls

"I love you. I hate you," said,
The whiskey and the rum
Which is it, my love?
Hate straight up
Or love on the rocks?

Goodbye to this Hurt Town
My heart isn't rent to own
Pain is in the squeaky floors
It's peeling off the walls
It's wailing through the open doors
I won't be taking your calls

They Sang the Horse Song

In your absence
They sang the Horse Song
I could not deny it
I danced it for me and for you

In your absence
They sang the Hummingbird Song
I could not deny it
I danced it for me and for you

In your absence
They sang the Star Song
I could not deny it
I danced it for me and for you

In your absence
They sang the Clan Song
I could not deny it
I danced it for mine and for yours

In your absence
They sang the Forever Song
I could not deny it

I truly danced alone.

Promises to Keep

We had some
Promises to keep
You kept one wing
I kept the other
So we would share the sky forever
We had some
Promises to keep
You held the moon
I held the sun
To guide us through darkness and the light
We had some
Promises to keep
You kept the water
I kept the fire
We had some
Promises to keep
You held the rainbow
I held the northern lights
We had some
Promises to keep
You held me
I held you
To keep away the cold, to hold in the warmth
We had some
Promises to keep
To stand on the earth
To hold up the sky
To remember the stars
To honour the moon
To praise the sun
We had some
Promises to keep

In Your Arms

In your arms
The troubles disappeared
I did not question your embrace
Your eyes became stars
Semaphores for refuge and dreams
Star Woman
I have not forgotten
The fire where our love was born
A signal fire for the sun
I have not forgotten
Waking to your face
At dawn
To prepare for our sunrise ceremony
Led by a spirit
That called out from the shoulders of the sun
I have not forgotten
Our silent glances across the flames
That flickered like sparks and met the sky
I have not forgotten
The smoke from the fire
Rising like prayers
I have not forgotten
The tobacco offered to the fire
For good life and love
I have not forgotten

You stared past the fire

You stared past the fire
Where this love began
You stared past the fire

You stared past the fire
Where once was forever
You stared past the fire

You stared past the fire
To where forever was elapsed
You stared past the fire

You stared past the fire
Once hallowed like love
You stared past the fire

You stared past the fire
To hallow firewater spirits
You stared past the fire

You stared past the fire
No longer perceived
You stared past the fire

Gatling Gun

You used a gatling gun
When a pistol would have done
You were always one
For extremes
I love you. I hate you
I admire you. I loathe you
I need you. I don't need you
I want you. I don't want you
Bullet-riddled and bleeding
I surrendered. I succumbed.

Permanent Scars

When you tore yourself from me
You left
Permanent scars
Another notch for you
Another silent lover
Left to heal alone
Heal alone
Permanent scar
Upon
Permanent scar

The Poem That Never Ends

When I was just a boy
I was just a boy
Curled in nests
Away from love
Away from you
The ones who tied my heart
Into knots too tight to be unbound

When I was just a boy
I was just a boy
Unable to tell
The difference between love and bondage
Away from love
Away from you
The ones who tied my soul
Into knots too tight to be unbound

When I was just a boy
I was just a boy
Unable to tell the difference between rope and ribbons
Away from love
Away from you
The ones who tied my hands
Into knots too tight to be unbound

When I was just a boy
When I was just a man

Ropes

I slept in nests
Of blood and grass and twigs
The sky my home
The highest apex I could find
Away from your reach
Away from ties that bound me
Away from older hands that swung tightly like ropes
Away from your long black hair
That hung in my face like the gallows

I slept in nests
Furled against the wind and rain
Gasping for sunlight
The small creek gurgling like a choking child

I flew away from all of you
Away from all of you,
makers of knots
That would not, could not, hold this bird,
This bird that learned to fly
With ropes that dangle
From the sky

The Bird Who Was Afraid To Fly

Chose to leave a darkened sky
Leaving the only place
He ever felt like a bird
The nest that never grew
Enough for deserting birds
To ever call home
Only became cluttered with every bit of detritus
The wind blew in
Bits of cloth and feathers and fallen leaves
The hoarded dust of years
Over-accumulated wounds
The cold wind numbed
Shaking his feathers of the gathering snow
The little bird
Looked back one more time
At the only place
He ever felt like a bird
Then flew

Someday I won't remember you

Someday
I won't know
Who you are
I will not
Remember you
You'll miss me then
When my memory
Is gone

Compass

I stay awake at night
So I don't have to dream of you
I'm going to stop
Wanting you all the time
In the upper reaches of the sky
There is another star
Waiting there
Not another heart
But a guiding light
Within another universe
Another constellation to set my compass by
Another way to navigate
Another way
From this unsettling dying star
That steals my sleep
And ends my dreams

Waiting for the Thunderbirds

Healing rain
Wash away this accumulated sorrow
This gathered pain
Fill this empty vessel
With your water and your light
Strike away these blues
Take them up and away, up and away
Open the barricades to heaven
And close the gates to hell

The Diet

These days devouring loss
The way a madman and a madwoman
Devour one another
Nothing satiates

I devour dreams
The way a madman and a madwoman
Devour one another's words and regret nothing
The crows are put to shame

I devour anger
The way a madman and a madwoman
Devour carrion of love and leave nothing to chance
The vultures are humbled

I devour grief
The way a madman and a madwoman
Devour the sun, the moon and the stars
The ravens and owls are chastened

I devour sadness
The way a madman and a madwoman
Devour the self from the inside out

Cannibals of love
A madman and a madwoman

Unwilling to offer, one to the other, I forgive you,
I love you

Come home.

Eyes wide open

I see. Love is so blind.

Yes, even with eyes wide open.

Yes, it's better to not rely on my eyes to see it.

What the eyes cannot see, the heart can see.

I hope my heart works.

If you are alive then there is love…

Sometimes I don't notice the love that I already have.

It's like the sun, always there, even when hidden by clouds.

I didn't notice until I was alone.

Sometimes we don't know what we have until it is far away and we find love to fill the empty space that we think is there, and we realize that love always makes room for more...

I miss you.

And, I miss you…

Far & Away

Lying flat on this stone
Spinning in the darkness
That star light fading
Light that seemed infinite
And forever
I cannot pretend

You are gone.

Evening Fuchsia

Flaming whiskey
stains the western sky
the fuchsia sun
lies
fallen
at your feet.

I am Beautiful in these Woods

I am once again beautiful in these woods
My heart mended by the poplar and the birch
The black spruce and the tamarack embrace me

Not knowing how to swim
You left me
I learned to hold my breath
Until I almost lost my skill to breathe

I retreated to the high granite and the jack pine
Reoriented to the horizons
I found my way again

Here in these woods, I am beautiful again
Here on these humble waters, I am beautiful again
I will drink that knowing
No one walks on water
They only think they do
I am once again beautiful on this earth

I Won't Be Calling

I won't be calling from a phone booth
From anywhere
Telling you that I miss you
While the rain falls
Under a barely discernible moon
Asking where the time went
I'll have no questions or pronouncements soaked with remorse
I won't be writing a letter on hotel stationary
From a lost hotel anywhere
These words are mine
Only my voice will be absent.

Broken Vows

I turned and watched you run
Back to where vows are easily broken
Without explanation or reason
Calling out your name
The wind carried it away

Let the moon tumble down
Let the stars fall
Let the sun burn out
Broken vows
Broken vows
Carried away by the wind
Tumbling down with the moon
Falling with the stars
Burning with the sun

I look out my window
I stare out my door
I came this far
Eighteen winters
To watch you leave.

Every Poem

Every poem I write
Ends with the same words
Even when they don't . . .
I miss you.

Death by a Thousand Poems

Words
Just words and thorns
Mine or yours
Absent of redemption or closure
Eulogies for love
Wound by seeping wound
Death by a thousand thorns
Death by a thousand poems
Our bodies of words
Epitaphs in weathered stone
Wispy as rain
Sink into the ground
Become
Thickets and bramble
Indistinguishable
One from the other
Death by a thousand thorns
Death by a thousand poems

Song for 1975

In the summer heat of seventeen

I flew into your sun

Cacophony ringing in my ears

I was in love with you

Beguiled by your songs

I fell from the sky

Begging for rain

Prairie

for Martha

There will be no going back. Even though a prairie of memory stretches as far as my memory can see, there shall be no return to our days in the grass, to our days of loving on the shore. The last time we spoke you gently reminded me to lay tobacco on the ground whenever I missed you. I knew you were saying goodbye.

A Greater Distance

for Alex

In the interstitial space
Between memory and loss
A greater distance
Than the distance between an unforgiving desert in
Mauritania
And here, this beloved, remembered lake in Minnesota
I miss you

To mark each summer that passes
I smoke a rolled American Spirit cigarette
In your honour
I light a fire on the shore
To light your way to me

Alexandra
There shall never be an absence of words or memories
or firewood
Of roll-your-owns, of love, or light, or laughter

There shall never be an absence of missing you.

Another Time

for MJR

First, I would give alms for the times I hurt you. I would make sure that the secret bird, the bird flute that I keep, makes its way back to you after I am gone, wrapped in purple ribbon for healing and redemption. Perhaps I would also send that wind and water swept stone that I have kept all these years, the one you pressed into my palm, a going away reminder of a once favoured shore. I would tell you why I left after the dream of the unassailable, impassable stone cathedral, how I tried to climb the jagged rocks that skirted it like a stone moat, and still could not reach you. I would listen to the song with the lyrics, "It's been 7 hours and 15 days…"

One second last time…

Nanokaasii

for Sandra

I found a hummingbird's nest
Tender and fragile as a whisper
Inside the miniature basket
Woven of tenderness and gossamer
Tiny fingers of light
Touched upon
A feather of yours
Love
Left behind
Still whispering inside of me

Semaphore

for Giizhigo-kwe

Sometimes questions are better left as questions because
then there will always be mystery. What is the universe
anyway, but a fire that began long ago? Questions are
better left as questions sometimes, to keep the flow of
love alive, then, there shall be no ending to the flames.
Flame to flame, entwined, flickering light in the
darkness, a semaphore when we need one, a place to
meet when the stars grow cold.

Other Lies

Secrets of the Stone

"The secret of two is God's secret, the secret of three is everybody's secret"
-Proverb

Attempting to bury secrets like stones
Those things that she had done
Not comprehending
The upward push of earth
Will bare stony secrets to the sky
To starlight and the moon
Blazing sun and cleansing rain
To sit again upon the earth
To once again
Be reckoned with
Be accounted for
Here I am
Gravity keeps me here.

I am going to drink

for the children of the 7th fire

I am going to drink
This poem tonight
All night, every night
I am going to drink
This poem tonight
This 100 proof poem
I am going to drink
This poem tonight
This weekend poem
I am going to drink
This poem tonight
This drunken love poem
I am going to drink
This poem tonight
This rum dumb poem
I am going to drink
This poem tonight
This beer piss poem
I am going to drink
This poem tonight
This smoky breath poem
I am going to drink
This poem tonight
This drunken lie poem
I am going to drink
This poem tonight
This 13th step poem
I am going to drink

This poem tonight
This easy poem
I am going to drink
This poem tonight
This black out poem
I am going to drink
This poem tonight
This nineteenth-hole poem
I am going to drink
This poem tonight
This flopping fish poem
I am going to drink
This poem tonight
This sprawled out poem
I am going to drink
This poem tonight
This gang bang poem
I am going to drink
This poem tonight
This belly up to the bar poem
I am going to drink
This poem tonight
This smoky bar poem
I am going to drink
This poem tonight
This passed out poem
I am going to drink
This poem tonight
This crying jag poem
I am going to drink

This poem tonight
This cry in my beer poem
I am going to drink
This poem tonight
This pissed off poem
I am going to drink
This poem tonight
This parking lot poem
I am going to drink
This poem tonight
This bar fight poem
I am going to drink
This poem tonight
This fuck him poem
I am going to drink
This poem tonight
This fuck me poem
I am going to drink
This poem tonight
This using poem
I am going to drink
This poem tonight
This getting used poem
I am going to drink
This poem tonight
This grief-stricken poem
I am going to drink
This poem tonight
This trauma filled poem
I am going to drink
This poem tonight
This cheating poem
I am going to drink
This poem tonight

This I owe you nothing poem
I am going to drink
This poem tonight
This you owe me nothing poem
I am going to drink
This poem tonight
This secret poem
I am going to drink
This poem tonight
This off with a bang poem
I am going to drink
This poem tonight
This drunken sex poem
I am going to drink
This poem tonight
This blow job poem
I am going to drink
This poem tonight
This truck sex poem
I am going to drink
This poem tonight
This car sex poem
I am going to drink
This poem tonight
This backseat poem
I am going to drink
This poem tonight
This hotel party poem
I am going to drink
This poem tonight
This hotel sex poem
I am going to drink
This poem tonight

This passed around poem
I am going to drink
This poem tonight
This forgotten poem
I am going to drink
This poem tonight
This forgotten children poem
I am going to drink
This poem tonight
This forgotten grandchildren poem
I am going to drink
This poem tonight
This lost memory poem
I am going to drink
This poem tonight
This poem will heal if you let it poem
I am going to drink
This poem tonight
This poem that doesn't forget
This poem
This poem
This poem

Also by Al Hunter:
– Poetry –

Spirit Horses – Kegedonce Press
The Recklessness of Love – Kegedonce Press